My Happy Book

Exodus 2:1–10
1 Samuel 1
Luke 2:1–20
Mark 10:13–16 for Children

Written by Gloria A. Truitt
Illustrated by Chris Sharp

ARCH ® Books
Copyright © 1995 Concordia Publishing House
3558 S. Jefferson Avenue, St. Louis, MO 63118-3968
Manufactured in the United States of America

THIS IS MY HAPPY BIRTHDAY BOOK

_____

PRESENTED BY

_____

DATE

_____

When Moses was just three months old,
His mother made a boat:
A basket boat she made from reeds,
And watertight to float.

She dressed her son in snuggly clothes
And saw to all his needs,
Then hid him near a riverbank,
Among the tall, thick reeds.

She did all this to save him from
A jealous, angry king,
Because great harm to her young child
She knew this king would bring.

The baby slept, safe in his boat,
Staying dry and warm,
While God watched over him with love
And kept him safe from harm.

Now God loves every child, and so
Of course, He loves you too ...
So just like Moses in the reeds,
He takes good care of you!

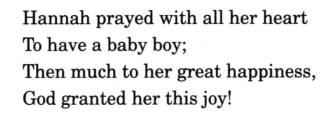

Hannah prayed with all her heart
To have a baby boy;
Then much to her great happiness,
God granted her this joy!

How thrilled she was when God gave her
A precious little son;
Samuel became God's messenger,
Was heard by everyone.

When he grew older he became
God's willing prophet and
Performed God's work throughout his years,
Just as his mother planned.

Just as Hannah taught her son
To pray to God each day,
The Lord gives you a special gift—
Grown-ups who teach His way.

Long ago in Bethlehem
A Child was born one day.
His birthplace was a stable and
His crib, a bed of hay.

God's angels sang His praises, and
The shepherds left their field
To find the newborn Son of God—
Beside this Child they kneeled.

Two thousand years have passed, but still
We celebrate His birth—
The baby Jesus sent by God
To save us all on earth.

Thank You, God, for sending us
The gift of Your true Son,
For Jesus is the greatest gift
You gave to everyone!

Long ago when Jesus preached,
The people gathered 'round.
And some brought children to be blessed,
But His disciples frowned.

They said that Jesus had no time
For children, young and small,
'Cause they were not important—
They were children, after all.

But Jesus heard and said to them,
"Please let them come to Me."
Then took them up and blessed them as
He held them on His knee.

It makes me feel so warm inside
To know that God is at my side.
I am so happy knowing He
Will always have His arms 'round me.

My birthday was a lot of fun,
With many games and prizes won!
I blew (*number*) candles out ... then YUM!
We ate the cake to the last crumb!

And now I'll say a thank-You prayer
For friends who took the time to share
An afternoon of fun and games.
See the last page to find their names!

The room seemed filled with presents that
I shook, then happily unwrapped.
Now, when I stop to think, I know
That as the years pass and I grow,
My *greatest* gift will always be
God's Son sent here for you and me!

Connect the dots
and draw the
candles on your
birthday cake.

These people helped
me celebrate: _____ _____

_____ _____

_____ _____

On my birthday,
I thank Jesus
for _____

_____

_____

This is my favorite
birthday present.